The Thoughtful Home

Dedication
to my darling Sassie

The Thoughtful Home

Creating a home
with heart
on any budget

Tahn Scoon

Photography by John Downs, Anastasia Kariofyllidis and Elouise van Riet-Gray

NH
NEW
HOLLAND

Contents

General Decorating Tips

Introduction

As a designer and magazine stylist, I've worked on some pretty incredible interiors, and have seen some of the loveliest homes imaginable.

Unfortunately, my own budget is nowhere near as big as either my clients or the homeowners whose houses we photograph.

Luckily, I don't think you necessarily need a lot of money to put together a really gorgeous interior. In fact, a lack of money can sometimes force you to be more creative. Some of the homes featured in this book have been decorated on very tight budgets.

I've included plenty of insider tips on how to style and decorate your home, as well as affordable decorating tricks and some super easy how-to projects to make. Hopefully, this will give you the knowledge to create your own truly beautiful interior.

A healthy home is a happy home, so I've also included suggestions on how to promote good air quality by selecting more eco-friendly materials and finishes.

I wish you all the best in creating a thoughtful, affordable and authentic home.

Happy Decorating

tahn scoon

Floor Treatments

Timber is my favourite choice for flooring. It is classified as a hard floor, so is appropriately hardy and easy to clean, but at the same time it has a certain amount of give, so is much more forgiving (on both children's knees and fine bone china) than tiles or concrete.

There are a number of ways to decorate timber floors, including re-staining, whitewashing, painting and stencilling. I just love the look of fresh white floors, which is why we've photographed so many of them, but be aware they do take a little more cleaning, as do black floors. If you have a lot of children, puppies or other messy creatures, or just don't like doing housework, mid brown-toned timber in a matt finish will be your best bet. Whichever finish you choose, don't forget there are always healthy, eco-friendly product options available.

You might think you're pretty much stuck with what you've got if you have dated tiles or carpeted floors, but I know one homeowner who had her tiles jack-hammered up and the concrete underneath polished. Another ripped up her dated blue carpet and painted the concrete slab in paving paint herself (see image opposite). If painted concrete isn't to your taste, and if your existing floor is in good shape, vinyl planks are an affordable and extremely easy DIY option as the planks can be laid straight on the concrete. For smaller spaces, you don't even need to use glue. However, vinyl is not an eco-friendly option, so my suggestion would be to pay a little extra to have underlay installed and then top with laminate, cork or bamboo.

Rug love

The pleasure of stepping onto a lush, hand-knotted wool rug is sublime. Be very generous with your sizing. Furniture, or at least the front feet of furniture, should sit on the rug. If the price of one large rug is prohibitive, layer a number of smaller rugs. Tactile, natural fibres are always visually better. If you can't afford wool, then sisal, hemp and jute are perfect and fit into almost any colourscheme.

Wall Treatments

Paint offers an easy and inexpensive method of adding colour and interest to walls. There are plenty of types and brands available ranging from natural distemper, which is a traditional chalk-based paint that leaves a 'mottled' velvety finish (most commonly seen in heritage homes), to high gloss enamel, which, with enough coats, produces a swish contemporary 'lacquered' effect (though the hardest, glossiest enamels are oil-based, so very chemically laden).

The most popular wall paint is semi-gloss water-based acrylic. It's affordable, easy to apply and readily available in healthier low-VOC (Volatile Organic Compound) varieties. If your ceilings aren't too high, painting walls is a job that you can easily do for yourself. The hardest part will be sorting through the plethora of colours on offer. If in doubt, I have found that a fresh, 'nearly' white is the way to go. It will lift both your room and your mood and will give you a perfect backdrop to decorate with.

You may like to add mouldings or timber cladding to plain plaster walls or shelving (as depicted opposite). A wide range of beautifully detailed skirting boards, dado and picture rails and cornices are all readily available from specialist timber suppliers and hardware stores, and are relatively easy to install (or have installed).

Another way to beautify walls is with wallpaper. The main choices are paper or vinyl. My inclination would be to choose paper as vinyl emits nasties, which may affect the air quality in your home. If you can, seek out companies that use water-based inks and sustainably sourced paper in their products. You can apply wallpaper yourself, though you'll need a certain skill base, a large table and other decorating equipment, so for a one-off project, it's probably best to call in a professional.

Temporary wallpapers on the other hand are very easy to apply as you simply peel and stick. They're completely removable, so perfect for renters or those who want to ring the changes quickly. I recommend non-vinyl, non-PVC options.

Window Treatments

Custom-made, professionally installed roman blinds or curtains that swish effortlessly along gliders are luxurious and perfect for homes that have a formal style setting a tone of grandeur. They often come with a similar price tag too. Here are some less expensive and more relaxed ideas:

Firstly, decide what you need. If you need daytime privacy, or you need to soften an unappealing view, but would still like to allow natural light to penetrate the room, then a sheer curtain (see page 96) will be perfect. You could also try a decorative window film, which is made to mimic exquisitely expensive frosted glass, at a fraction of the cost (see opposite).

If, however, you need full privacy, particularly in the evenings and at night, and to block out street- or sun-light, you'll need heavier curtains, perhaps even lined in block-out fabric (a product that is great for young children's bedrooms). Ready-made curtains can be purchased to fit specific window heights and widths and the hem turned up as appropriate. You may also be able to find good quality pre-loved curtains online for a fraction of the price of new.

When buying pre-made curtains, the trick is to measure the drop well. Take the measurement from the top of the rod to the floor. You'll need to buy curtains at least this long. You can always turn up a hem if they're too long (by machine if you sew, or with no-sew hemming tape, if the curtain fabric isn't too heavy). You'll also need to measure the width and ensure the curtains are wide enough to cover your window, with plenty to spare. A generous quantity of curtain fabric creates a sense of luxury.

Alternatively, if you have standard size windows, ready-made blinds are another affordable option. They're easy to install but only available in limited sizes. Plantation shutters are a coveted option but quite expensive: a little tip is to order white venetian blinds, specifying extra wide blands (at least 60 mm). This will give you a similar look at around a third of the price.

As for hardware, regular rods are probably the easiest to install and most versatile to use as you can attach curtains in many ways, including via eyelets, tabs, ties or a simple rod pocket (see page 96).

Looking at Storage

Creating good storage isn't the most exciting and glamorous of decorating topics but if addressed correctly it will probably make the biggest difference to how you live in and enjoy your home on a daily basis. If you've ever lived in a home with no storage (perhaps a cute, little cottage with only a scant number of kitchen cupboards and a couple of freestanding robes) you'll know how frustrating it can be when there's nowhere to put your belongings. While we can take a leaf out of our grandmothers' books and live with less stuff, we also need to create clever, user-friendly storage for the belongings we do need.

While I generally advocate vintage furniture, in the case of storage it's not always the most effective and user-friendly. A lot of space in a room tends to get wasted around free-standing pieces, whereas bespoke built-in cabinetry can be designed to fit into any nook and utilise any available space. There's also the matter of lovely soft-closing drawers over sticky old runners!

The downside to custom cabinetry is the relatively high cost. A way around this is to install inexpensive flat-pack shelving and then 'build it in' by way of adding timber framing or cladding. It'll create a more bespoke look on a DIY budget.

When planning large-scale storage, take the opportunity to really think about what you specifically need to store, and design accordingly. Common, but often forgotten, items include phone chargers and remotes, children's school bags and homework notes, basic household tools, and craft and gift-wrapping supplies. Open shelving is perfect for housing neat rows of books or a collection of ceramics. Closed storage, by way of cupboards and drawers, will be better for messier, less-uniform items. There is also the option of open shelving, concealed by full-sized sliding doors.

Peace and Quiet

Most of us desire peace and quiet for at least some of the time in our homes, so if you have excessive internal or external noise, the following measures may help:

Internal noise is most often an issue when there are too many hard surfaces, such as timber floors, stone bench tops and tiled walls. Sounds can be softened, or 'absorbed', to some degree by adding soft furnishings. Try layering thick wool rugs over bare floors, cover windows with heavy fabric roman blinds or curtains rather than rollers or shutters and choose upholstered furniture over hard.

External noise most often comes from traffic or neighbours. Insulating your walls will offer the most protection Take care to seal any gaps in window and door frames and consider replacing regular glass with treated. Noise bounces off hard surfaces but will be absorbed to some extent by soft surfaces, so think about replacing external paved surfaces with grass or ground cover. If it's traffic noise that is bothering you, it's tempting to put up a solid rendered fence but this sometimes creates a tunnelling effect, with noise seeping in through the gate. Instead, try a three-tiered planting approach composed of ground cover, hedging and some taller shrubs or trees. This will also have the added benefit of filtering traffic pollution.

Looking at Lighting

A welcoming home has an abundance of good natural daylight. If your home doesn't receive enough, consider installing a skylight, replacing heavy drapes for sheers, or a small window for French doors. Take a look at your internal doors. Sometimes you can 'steal' light from a sun-soaked room by replacing regular doors with glazed or louvered options, allowing light into areas that might not usually receive it (see opposite).

Conversely, in warmer climates, sunlight may be too strong, causing glare. Filter with treated glazing, translucent blinds or sheer curtains. The desire for light must always be tempered with the desire to stay cool for those in hot climates, or stay warm for those in colder climates. The trick is to establish where light, heat and draughts enter your home and dress windows and doors accordingly.

Artificial lighting

To achieve beautifully lit rooms by way of artificial lighting, the trick is to layer your light. Avoid relying on one central pendant in a room; the single pool of downlight it creates leaves corners in the dark, which makes a room appear smaller and less inviting. Add wall lights, table and floor lamps and even candles to create overlapping pools of light, right into the corners. Rows of downlights are handy in kitchens and bathrooms but avoid them in other rooms as they're neither aesthetically pleasing nor flattering.

A single source of light may create glare, presenting too much contrast between lit and unlit areas. This is true whether the source of light is a lamp or a television screen. Again, create overlapping pools of light by incorporating multiple light sources.

Working with Mirrors

I love, love mirrors. They bounce light around a room, making it appear lighter, brighter and more spacious than it is, so they're great for all rooms, but especially those with small or minimal windows. Generously sized vintage Venetian mirrors are a favourite, as they lend a pleasing impression of glamour, but as with all large mirrors, they're incredibly expensive.

A cheaper way to obtain a large mirror is to commission your local glazier to supply you with a mirror cut to size and have it mounted directly to the wall. You could then commission a handyperson to build a frame around the mirror and attach this directly to the wall too. Your choice of frame can be anything, from simple plain timber to a more detailed architrave, both will be available from your local hardware store – and can be painted or stained in any colour (see image opposite).

Another inexpensive option is to source a second hand mirror and revamp the frame. I recently bought a huge silky-oak framed mirror at a charity store for next to nothing. It was originally designed to sit above a fireplace but with a fresh coat of white paint it will make an amazing hall mirror.

Generally you'll find smaller, rather than larger, vintage mirrors in charity stores. Amass a collection and hang as a group for greater impact. One of our homeowners cleverly mounted a collection of affordable frameless art deco mirrors in lieu of a new splashback (see page 33).

New or Vintage?

What to buy new:

Fresh white linen sheets (old sheets will never be a lovely pure white).
A white porcelain dinner set (white is best for displaying food)
A stainless cutlery set (vintage silver is prettier but requires high maintenance cleaning)
A good quality mattress
A good quality sofa

What to buy vintage:

Pretty vintage quilts (small print florals)
Fine bone china (in pretty patterns; perfect for afternoon tea parties)
Vintage cutlery
Bed frames and headboards
Hard furniture (it can always be revamped)

Tips for buying vintage furniture

Check items are structurally sound. Colours and fabrics can be updated easily, but you don't want to be fixing the actual piece. You also can't change the shape of an item, so make sure you love it.

When buying drawers, check the runners. If they're only a little bit sticky, rub a little soap or candle wax over them and they should glide more easily. But if the drawers are really hard to open and close, it may be best to give that particular piece of furniture a miss—runners are quite costly to replace.

Don't buy anything that may have been painted in lead paint, which was in use up until the 1970s. If you're unsure, buy a cheap colour-change test kit from your local hardware store. Don't be scared off by this! Remember, most things available to us now were made after the 1970s. Very old antiques are also perfectly fine as they're usually finished in a natural product such as shellac or beeswax.

What to take shopping:

• The measurements of the space that you have available to fit the item: you don't want to cart something home that doesn't fit in the designated space, so measure carefully first.
• Samples: paint chips, fabric cuttings, tile and any timber samples you may need to match.
• A camera: take photographs of any items you're considering, to look at later. It can also be a good idea to take a photo of the pricetag
• A photograph of the space you're decorating: it'll help you to keep focused.

Looking at Colour

WARM IT UP:

Rather than using stark black and white schemes, use warm chocolate-charcoals and warm creamy whites instead. Your interiors will instantly feel more refined and welcoming.

CHECK YOUR UNDERTONES:

For harmonious schemes, ensure colours share the same undertones. This is especially important when working with neutral and natural palettes. For example, white with grey undertones won't look good against cream with yellow undertones.

LOOK TO MOTHER NATURE:

Depending on the quality of light your home receives, a pure white may be too stark for exteriors. Use earthier shades such as soft greens, stony greys and rich creams instead, all of which look beautiful with a fresh white trim.

USE ONE WHITE FOR INTERIORS:

If it is a deeper white, use full strength for walls, half for trims and quarter for ceilings. If it's a lighter white, use the same colour for all surfaces. You'll still get some variation due to the different gloss strengths required for each surface.

PLAY WITH DEPTH:

If you're using a lot of the same colours, say greys and taupes, create more interest by varying the depth. For example, a mid-taupe sofa could be teamed with a charcoal rug and soft grey walls.

Furnishing Rooms Thoughtfully

Hallways

Hallways and entries often become the unofficial dumping ground for a host of unattractive items, including grubby shoes, schoolbags and umbrellas, so make sure you incorporate plenty of storage into the space if you can. A bespoke built-in cupboard is ideal if space and budget allow, otherwise consider free-standing cupboards, a box to contain shoes, coat hooks and/or an umbrella stand, all of which will help you to keep clutter off the floor.

Using the walls of the hallway as a space to display photographs or pictures is popular, though your space needs to be wide enough to allow you to can stand back and see the images clearly. In narrow, darker hallways, mirrors thoughtfully placed will enhance the sense of space, and reflect, and therefore multiply, any available light.

To keep noise down and create softness underfoot, consider a hall runner. A plush wool runner is perfect or you could try a less expensive natural sisal runner instead. If it's colour and pattern you're after, buy four or five inexpensive cotton mats and stitch them together to create one long runner.

You could also freshen a staircase by adding a new runner. Again, sisal is a good choice and goes with almost any décor. Alternatively, you may like to repaint in a striking hue, or try something more fun, such as wallpapered risers.

Lastly, make sure you add something spectacular, such as an oversized vintage print, an ornate Venetian mirror or an antique chandelier dripping in crystals.

Kitchens

If you're installing a new bespoke kitchen, ask the cabinetmaker to use EO MDF. It looks the same as regular MDF, but it is a healthier and more eco-friendly choice. You might even like to investigate plywood or recycled timber. If you'd like to team cabinets with engineered stone, try a more environmental option, such as those made from recycled glass, mirror and porcelain.

The most affordable choice for bench tops will be laminate. Stone will be the most expensive. Keep the price down a little by purchasing direct from a stonemason, rather than through a cabinetmaker or kitchen retailer.

On the other hand, if you're purchasing a kitchen 'off the shelf' why not look at secondhand options, or ask your local kitchen retailer if they might sell you an old display kitchen. New flatpack kitchens are, of course, a great option and are available from IKEA and all your major hardware stores. The trick to a successful install is to have someone check your walls and floor levels before installation.

If, however, you've inherited an old kitchen that is functional and structurally sound but perhaps not to your taste, save yourself money by retaining the layout, plumbing and carcasses and concentrate on making some cosmetic updates. Doors can be replaced or painted; handles, taps and pendants upgraded; new granite set over existing bench tops and new splashback tiles over old (as long as the old tiles are in good enough condition).

The thing common to all kitchens is they contain a lot of hard surfaces, so the trick to decorating them successfully is to add softness. Consider fabric roman blinds instead of rollers or shutters, upholstered or woven stools, fabric pendants, a lush plant and a cotton or sisal floor runner.

Dining Rooms

Commissioning a quality bespoke table is surprisingly often cheaper than buying a ready-made mid- to high-end designer table off the shelf. The benefits include being able to select your own timber, colour stain and size; the latter consideration is of particular benefit if you have an unusually narrow or awkward space.

Alternatively, the most cost-effective way to buy a quality timber table is to source one from a charity store or salvage yard. As long as the structure is sound and you love the shape, you can always revamp the colour or stain. Whitewashing or waxing are all that's required if you're after a relaxed, provincial feel, or try a high gloss finish for a more contemporary look.

The most comfortable dining chairs are generally upholstered. If your budget doesn't stretch to buying new, buy second hand and make or buy new fitted slipcovers. Woven armchairs are also very comfortable, if they're well cushioned. They can be bought new, or you could pick up vintage ones and furnish them with fluffy new cushions.

If you want to spend as little money as possible, source a selection of old timber chairs and repaint them. Even if they are all different, you can unify them with paint colour (though sometimes they look better mismatching). Alternatively, you may be able to cover a set of dated chairs with inexpensive slipcovers.

Top it all off (literally) with a truly spectacular light fitting. While vintage crystal chandeliers and high-end contemporary designs are deservedly drool-worthy, the price tag can be a little hefty. Fortunately, you can always make your own (with the help of an electrician, which you'll need for installation anyway). Cloches, vintage jars, timber bowls and even crystal decanters (see page 112) can all be turned into pendants.

Alternatively, you may already have a tired but well-shaped fitting, in this case consider repainting it (see page 115).

Living Rooms

A good sofa is a must have for a living room. Whilst a new high-quality sofa is ideal, it's a fairly substantial investment.

Fortunately, you can always source a decent second-hand sofa and have it re-covered. Reupholstering is a great solution but can be expensive. Custom-fitted slipcovers are miles cheaper (for the best price, try a specialist sewing service rather than an upholsterer).

Alternatively, purchase an affordable new sofa from IKEA and order bespoke slipcovers, which are readily available through specialist on-line stores in a wide range of fabrics.

Ornate vintage pieces, with their intricate shapes, can be hard to fit slipcovers to and expensive to upholster. You may be able to freshen them by simply updating the seat cushions. It'll be near impossible to match old fabric; try a plain linen (see opposite) or simple ticking stripe instead.

As for hard furniture, buy affordable raw pine side and coffee tables and revamp with a lick of paint. Quality vintage pieces can receive the same treatment.

Underfoot, heavy, hand-knotted wool rugs feel the most luxurious. If the price is prohibitive, sisal and hemp are well priced and go with almost any interior.

Open-Plan Living

Open-plan living provides a greater sense of spaciousness, better airflow and allows more light to pour into our homes. Visually, we share space with others more often, which is conducive to both socialising and watching over our families. For most of us, it's our preferred way to live. However, when not designed well, it can lack warmth and a sense of intimacy.

Good open-plan designs will architectural features, such as bulkheads, steps and partial walls that serve to break the space into 'rooms'. If this isn't the case, and you're faced instead with one large unbroken space (and often an uninspiring expanse of white walls and white kitchen cabinetry), you can delineate the space and add interest with clever decorating.

The first thing to do is to define each 'room' by using rugs, pendant lighting and large furniture. A large area rug works particularly well in the living space. It needs to be big enough so at least the front legs of all furniture can be placed on it. Aesthetically, a generous rug under the dining table also works well, but as it's trickier to clean than hard floors, you may prefer to have an eye-catching pendant instead as the focal point. Freestanding bookcases or sideboards may also help to separate areas.

Another option is to define spaces with paint colour or wallpaper. Keep in mind, this works best on walls that are an architectural feature in their own right, as the paint or paper needs a natural place to start and stop.

Once each space has been defined, it's time to decorate. When you do, approach each area as if it's a single room. Soften the hard surfaces of the kitchen, for example, with linen blinds or upholstered barstools. Add interest with wallpaper, unusual tiles or chalkboard paint. The dining area is often small but make a statement by repainting the chairs in a contrasting colour and installing a spectacular light fitting. Make the living room as inviting as possible by layering soft wool throws and feather cushions on linen sofas. Add ottomans, side tables and lamps.

Ensure colours are complementary, but not perfectly matching to keep each area as its own entity. Noise and mess can be an issue in open plan design. Soften noise by adding wool rugs, upholstered furniture and fabric window treatments. Wool rugs, upholstered furniture and fabric blinds and curtains will do much to soften noise. Good storage will ensure that clutter is kept minimal.Custom built-in cabinetry generally works best, as does regular de-cluttering!

Bedrooms

The bed is usually the most expensive item in a bedroom. The mattress should be new and the best quality that you can afford. What fills the mattress greatly determines the comfort and price. At the luxurious end of the market, mattresses may be filled with silk, wool and cashmere. At the lower end, filling may consist of low-grade foams and cotton and coconut fibres. A mattress also needs to be aired regularly (so despite what our mothers told us, it's actually good to not make your bed sometimes!), and replaced around every ten years.

The bed frame, however, can be purchased second hand. Antique wrought iron frames often look adorable as is. Dated timber frames though, may need a helping hand. Maybe give them a new lease of life with a coat of high gloss paint. Revamp upholstered bed heads with a piece of fabric that co-ordinates with the look of the room and a staple gun, or if you're handy with a sewing machine, make a simple fitted slipcover.

New bedside tables are often expensive. Buy vintage instead. They don't even need to match. You might like to choose a cupboard or drawers for practicality, on one side and an appealing little table on the other. For a sense of harmony, match heights to your bed.

Side lighting is much more relaxing than overhead lighting, so you'll definitely want some bedside lamps in a bedroom. Make sure they're well shaded so you're not subject to glare. Vintage bases are beautiful (though check they're electrically sound) and can be teamed with a fabric shade of your choice (see page 112).

And, a note on flooring: most of us love the feel of soft carpet underfoot when we step out of bed, but I believe hard floors with large area rugs look better (and you can take them with you if you move). If you can't afford a large area rug, buy a number of small rugs and have them sewn together 'patchwork' style (this works best with patterned rugs).

Children's Rooms

Feature wallpaper

Add instant drama with a papered wall. Feature walls generally work wonderfully in kids' rooms, in fact wallpapering all four walls may be too much (design and cost wise), so one wall is perfect. For longevity, bypass the children's prints and go with a more grown-up design, such as a geometric trellis or a vintage floral. Alternatively, try one of the new temporary wallpapers.

Mix and match fabrics

Oh, I love this, especially in a little girl's room. When choosing all the bedding, curtains and other soft furnishings, gather together a super sweet mix of small and large print florals, stripes and geometrics and toss them all in together 'cottage garden' style. To create an adorable mix, as opposed to a mess, keep your backdrop neutral (white preferably).

Vintage pieces

From an adorable bedside repainted in a soft shade and given a set of fresh crystal knobs, to an old dresser revamped in high gloss stripes or a battered industrial locker left as is, vintage furniture brings heart and soul, and a big dollop of individuality to any child's room.

Multi-colour schemes

Rethink safe two or three colour palettes and go for a less predictable multi-colour scheme instead. Start with a neutral base, such as white or charcoal and then add a medley of colours.

The trick is to use colours in the same tonal range. Try a delicious assortment of gelato-inspired hues on a fresh white base, 'worn' vintage shades on soft white or strong citrus tones on a charcoal backdrop.

The **Pink Ballet Slippers**

A Junior Career Story

EVELYN S. DERKES

Bathrooms

If you're renovating an older bathroom, you'll almost always save a lot of money by leaving the plumbing and services where they are and working within the existing layout (the exception may be if you have a home in which the plumbing is easy to access).

If you're on a really tight budget, only replace what you really need, and paint the rest. Cabinet doors, basins, baths, tiles and even grout can be repainted, and you can save a lot of money by painting rather than tiling walls. You will, of course, need to use the correct paints (and primers) for the specific jobs, but your local paint store will be happy to help you with that.

When choosing your colour scheme, if in doubt stick to a simple white colour palette. It will never date and, if done well, can look more expensive than it is, especially if teamed with higher quality fittings, which can be sourced inexpensively online.

A simple white bathroom is the perfect base from which to decorate. With just a few cosmetic changes you can create something quite spectacular. Try adding one striking pendant, an oversized ornate mirror (in lieu of a plain bathroom mirror), one designated section of feature tile, an irreverent artwork, a patterned shower curtain (though never use vinyl for health reasons) and/or a coloured or patterned roman blind.

Don't be afraid to do something quite unexpected, such as repaint your bath in a bold hue and then add a contemporary chandelier. Be aware though, a chandelier (or any light fitting) can only be installed over a bath if you're ceilings are high enough. Check with your electrician.

Home Offices

Good storage is key to having a well-functioning, practical work space, so that needs to be addressed first. If built-in storage isn't available, flat-pack storage will suffice. Generally I prefer to furnish a home with vintage furniture, though in an office it doesn't always provide the uniformity and usability you might need (depending on what you do).

Consider buying flat-pack storage second hand, the big brand pieces hold their value well, so you mightn't save much on the actual price, but you'll save yourself on the task of assembly.

Once storage is under control, the next step is to assess how you work. If you need visual clarity and a sense of order, keep your scheme neutral—all white is the most serene—and contain any colour and chaos. Consider mounting an antique frame to house any inspirational images or notes. For others, being surrounded by all that is inspirational and well loved contributes to creativity. In this case, an entire wall may be your moodboard!

My other tip is to invest in a decent chair. If you spend a lot of time sitting at your desk, you don't want to be sitting on an industrial metal chair, no matter how good it looks. At the very least, source a comfortable upholstered chair. If you require even more back support…but don't like the look of ergonomic design…, you can always take a tip from the Swedes and update it with a linen slipcover.

Small Spaces

A small home means a small footprint, which is an incredibly thoughtful way to live. Sometimes we get carried away with the idea that we need a bigger house, but perhaps we just need to learn to live better in the home we have. Small can be incredibly beautiful, and liberating, we just need to adjust our decorating approach a little.

The first step is to de-clutter. Be ruthless and let go of everything you don't need. Remember, a lot of things we hang onto 'in case we need it one day' are easily replaceable should that day ever come. We don't need to own everything; power tools can be hired and library books borrowed. You'll feel much more relaxed in a small space if you have room to breathe.

Next implement really good storage. This usually means built-in storage. For the purposes of small spaces freestanding pieces lend visual bulkiness, are often too deep and create unusable space to the sides of them. In contrast, built-in storage can be as sleek and streamlined as you desire, and can make the most of any available space. Consider bookshelves under the stairs or a study nook on the landing.

In larger rooms, devote an entire wall to storage. This will ultimately be less obtrusive and more practical than taking a piecemeal approach to storing and displaying objects. The storage may be a statement piece combining closed storage with open display shelving, or it may be flush floor-to-ceiling closed cabinetry, which almost reads as a wall.

Whilst some designers successfully work with a dark, moody palette to enhance the cocooning effect of a small space, if a sense of largeness is what you desire, white is a better choice. Whites, and hues that contain a lot of white, reflect light and bounce it about the room, visually expanding the space.

Try a light creamy white to lighten up a home that doesn't receive enough sun, and a deeper grey-white to cool down a home that receives too much. Keep an all-white colour scheme interesting by layering it with natural textures, such as lime-washed oak floors, stone bench tops and linen upholstery.

If you'd like to introduce some colour, cool colours recede, making them less dominant and more relaxing to live with. Try blues and the cooler shades of green. Light blues and greens work particularly well as they reflect light as well as recede, promoting a greater sense of spaciousness and serenity.

However, you don't need to forgo stronger, brighter colours if that's your preference; just use them more sparingly. For example, rather then wallpapering an entire apartment in a sunny yellow print, select just one feature wall or one small self-contained room (perhaps a powder room or child's bedroom), and ensure the background colour of the paper is white so it blends with the remaining walls.

If you're building or renovating, specify higher than conventional doorways to create the perception of height, and higher ceilings to add volume. In newer homes, keep architectural details to a minimum. Fussy details such as ornate skirting, cornices and picture rails will make a room feel smaller. In the interests of retaining clean lines, you may even consider adding a shadow gap in lieu of conventional skirting board. In older homes, it is advisable to retain original architectural features, but minimise their impact by painting them in the same colour as the wall.

Ensure your home receives adequate natural daylight. If it doesn't, consider replacing a too-small window with a more generous one, or installing skylights to internal rooms. (Ensure you have sufficient protection from the elements though).

Window treatments are best kept simple; try tailored linen roman blinds or sheer white curtains. White plantation shutters are a visually appealing option, though they take up a little more room. If you can't sacrifice the budget or space needed for shutters, try high-end white timber blinds for a similar look (ask for extra wide blades).

Furniture should be simple with low, clean lines. Less is more in a smaller home. Only buy what you need and ensure it is appropriately sized by measuring the space carefully. Be cautiously generous with main items such as sofas; one larger piece will look better than lots of small, dainty pieces. Keep in mind, custom-made furniture is not always more expensive than store bought, when of a comparative quality. It may be worth commissioning a narrower than standard dining table to save a few precious inches of walkway.

For those smaller pieces of furniture, try Perspex, glass and mirrored furniture for their respective transparent and reflective qualities. In addition, oversized wall-mounted mirrors will be hugely beneficial, especially when positioned to reflect a pleasing external view.

Floors are best pale and continuous. However, if you'd prefer to change materials, for example, from timber in the living area to tiles in the bathroom, simply select tiles in a colour close to the timber stain. As in every design and finish decision in a small home; the idea is to keep the colour palette calm, lines clean and visual clutter to a minimum.

Tips for Renters

Start with a fresh white base. If you don't have one, seek permission to repaint the walls. Most property owners will be open to this suggestion, especially if you're willing to share or cover the cost.

Take a look at your light fittings. If they're stock standard and completely uninspiring, change the shades. This is a simple job that you can do for yourself. However, if you want to change the wiring, you'll need to call in an electrician. Because of the cost, this is better only for long-term rentals.

If unattractive floors are your problem, layer with area rugs. Invest in generously sized hand-knotted wool rugs if your budget allows, or go for smaller cotton and sisal rugs and layer them if you need to keep costs down.

If window treatments are functional but uninspiring, perhaps plain roller or vertical blinds, retain them for their usability but add a rod and sheer curtain to beautify the window area. Alternatively, replace treatments altogether. Make a simple little curtain or buy affordable white timber venetian blinds, or similar, from your local hardware store and install them yourself. This is an easy DIY job as the blinds will come with brackets and screws, you'll only need access to a cordless drill.

Decorate walls by propping up large artworks, hanging smaller pieces with removable self-adhesive hooks, installing temporary wallpaper or decals, or seeking permission to install additional picture hooks.

Note: always seek written permission before making any changes.

Style Like a Pro

When styling a home in preparation for a magazine shoot, here are a few of the things we look at:

What to highlight

- Drop-dead gorgeous furniture, especially vintage or bespoke pieces.
- Really lovely designer fabrics, in cushions, curtains and other soft furnishings.
- A home's ability to receive quality natural light.
- How comfortable and inviting a home might be—if it has little spots you just want to ensconce yourself in.

What to hide

We tend to remove, hide or at least not draw attention to:

- Appliances—hard to do a daily basis unless you have a designated cupboard or pantry.
- Televisions—don't draw attention to your TV by having all your furniture directed towards it.
- Excess cords—if this is your problem, try an inexpensive cable tidy.
- Dated aluminium window frames—soften any unattractive window frames with sheer linen or cotton curtains.
- Unfashionable floors—layer dated tiles or carpeted floors in lovely rugs.

What to add

Common props that help to make a home feel more welcoming are:

- Flowers! Just because they're beautiful.
- Cushions and throws — to 'break up' sofas and beds and to make them feel more inviting.
- White linen—fresh white towels, bed and table linen lift almost any home.
- A designer handtowel to add colour and pattern to a contemporary bathroom.
- A pretty tea towel—especially lovely in an all-white kitchen.
- A pretty teacup and a pile of books—to make you want to sit a while.
- Rugs and sheepskins—to break up large expanses of floor.

These ideas might help you look at your own home with fresh eyes and see if there's any styling steps you can take to help present it at its most appealing.

It's also interesting to note, the homes that look the best (in print and real life) are those that have a very clear, individual sense of style, which is carried right through the home, even into oft-forgot spots such as the powder room and laundry area.

How to display

Collections
- Group like with like (for example, all white ceramics).
- Layer heights and types (tallest vessels with shorter vessels, handmade with off-the-shelf, new with vintage).
- Add something unexpected (a contemporary lipstick pink resin vessel).

Assorted Pieces
- Find something, however subtle, to pull items together. It could be a colour, shape, texture or purpose.
- Group in odd numbers and vary the heights. Place the taller item first and cluster the others around it.
- If a collection of items looks too messy, consider housing them in a container, vessel or on a tray.
- Most importantly, only display what you love.

House Plants

House plants have made a comeback, which is a good thing for the thoughtful home. Plants literally add life and colour to a room and absorb pollutants, thereby improving the air quality in your home.

House plants, especially when used in kitchens and bathrooms, tend to break up huge expanses of tile in a very organic way. The other thing I love about house plants is they have this ability to mimic the natural greenery you may have outside, and visually 'bring it in'.

Some of the best house plants to choose, in terms of their ability to soak up pollutants, are the peace lily, kentia palm and rubber plant.

Inside Outside

Decorating needn't stop at your front door. Create little sitting nooks and larger entertaining areas in your garden and on your deck or patio, and decorate in much the same way as you would inside—with comfortable furniture, soft furnishings and lighting.

Old timber furniture that looks a little dated can be given a new lease of life with a fresh coat of paint and some new cushions. Ensure paint is water-based as enamel has a tendency to peel in the sun, and ensure you use outdoor fabrics and inserts for your cushions so they don't fade or become mouldy. Fresh white paint teamed with green and white fabrics are a perennial favourite!

Clever planting can make outdoor rooms even more enjoyable to be in. Plant a deciduous tree in the perfect spot to provide shade in summer and allow for sun in winter. If insects are a problem, try tansy and mint to repel ants, and the herb rue to deter flies and mosquitoes (an outdoor ceiling fan will help too). If you like to entertain in the evenings, consider planting night Jasmine so your guests can delight in its delicious scent.

Easy How-To
Projects

Bed Linen Detail

For luxury designer-style bed linen without the price tag, simply add an embroidered or lace trim to plain sheets and pillowcases.

Adding a trim to sheets

You'll need a trim just a little longer than the width of your sheet, a flat sheet and a sewing machine.

1. Turn in a hem on one short edge of the trim by hand.
2. Starting at the hemmed edge of the trim, pin the trim along the top of the topside of the sheet. Machine-sew along the entire length of the trim to secure it to the sheet.
3. Hem the second short edge of the trim by hand.

Adding a trim detail to a pillowcase

You'll need a trim just a little longer than the height of your pillowcase, a pillowcase and a sewing machine.

1. Hem the short edges of the trim by hand.
2. Carefully unstitch the top seam on the front of the pillowcase, from edge to edge.
3. Slip your trim into the unpicked seam.
4. Re-sew.

Note: for easy care, ensure your trim is machine washable.

Magazine Bedside

For a super quick bedside, perhaps for last-minute guests, simply stack piles of magazines to the desired height and secure firmly with belts.

We've used two belts, which were bought inexpensively from an op shop, and belted them together first (to create enough length) before strapping them around the magazines.

Envelope Cushion

Envelope cushions are incredibly easy to make, as they don't require a zip—it's just one piece of material with seams stitched in the right places. The measurements here are for a standard 45 cm/18 in square cushion, however, you can always adjust to make any size you desire.

You'll need just 1 metre/1¼ yards of fabric and a sewing machine.

1. Cut a piece of fabric 100 x 50 cm/40 x 20 in. Run a 1 cm/½ in seam around the entire piece.
2. Place on a flat surface with the right side up.
3. Fold the top end down and the bottom end up, overlapping them in the middle—adjusting until the folded cushion is approx 45 cm/17 in long. Pin the entire length of each side and sew.
4. Turn right side out.
Note: 1 metre/1¼ yards of fabric will make two cushions.

Embroidered Heart

1. To create an embroidered heart detail, simply download a heart template (readily available online) and print it out.
2. Pin the heart template onto the cushion front.
3. Using embroidery thread (for the thickness) and a large sewing needle, sew around the outline in a simple running stitch.
4. Once you're finished, carefully tear away the paper.

Cutting Cushions

Designer fabric cuttings can be ordered online for next to nothing and can be patched together to create designer-look cushions for a fraction of the price.

Collect as many cuttings as it takes to create a piece of fabric approximately 100 x 50cm/40 x 20 in, and then follow the instructions on how to make an Envelope Cushion.

Note: You can patch your fabrics together in the regular basic square method or, as most cuttings are already over locked; you might want to sew them together in a more contemporary overlapping style (as shown).

Patchwork Silk Throw

I was lucky to receive a sample book of discontinued fabrics, which I cut up and used as my squares for this patchwork throw. However, patchwork can be made from any fabric remnants new or used.

To make a similar throw, with a finished size approximately 150 cm/60 in, you will need, 16 squares each 40 x 40cm/16 x 16 in, a backing fabric (I used ticking) approximately 160 x 160 cm/63 x 63 in, and a sewing machine.

1. Cut all the patchwork pieces to a uniform size.
2. Arrange the squares on the floor to create the design you desire.
3. Pin the squares into horizontal rows and sew the patches together into rows (there will be four rows).
4. Pin each row together aligning the seams and sew (the front of your throw is now complete).
5. Trim the backing fabric so it's the same size as the patchwork piece.
6. Place right sides together and pin along three sides, leaving one narrow end open.
7. Sew the three pinned sides together.
8. Turn right side out.
9. Sew the open end shut (tucking under the edges to keep them neat).

Hessian Tablecloth

The wonderful thing about hessian (burlap) is it's unbelievably cheap and comes in an extra-generous 180 cm/70 in width, making it perfect for tablecloths.

1. Cut a piece of fabric to the length of your table, plus overhang and then add a striped bias trim all around the edge. If you're an experienced sewer, you could mitre the corners. However, for beginners, simply cut four lengths of bias to match the four sides of the cloth and sew to the fabric in four straight seams, overlapping the trim at each end.

Note: Find a bias trim that doesn't fray too much.

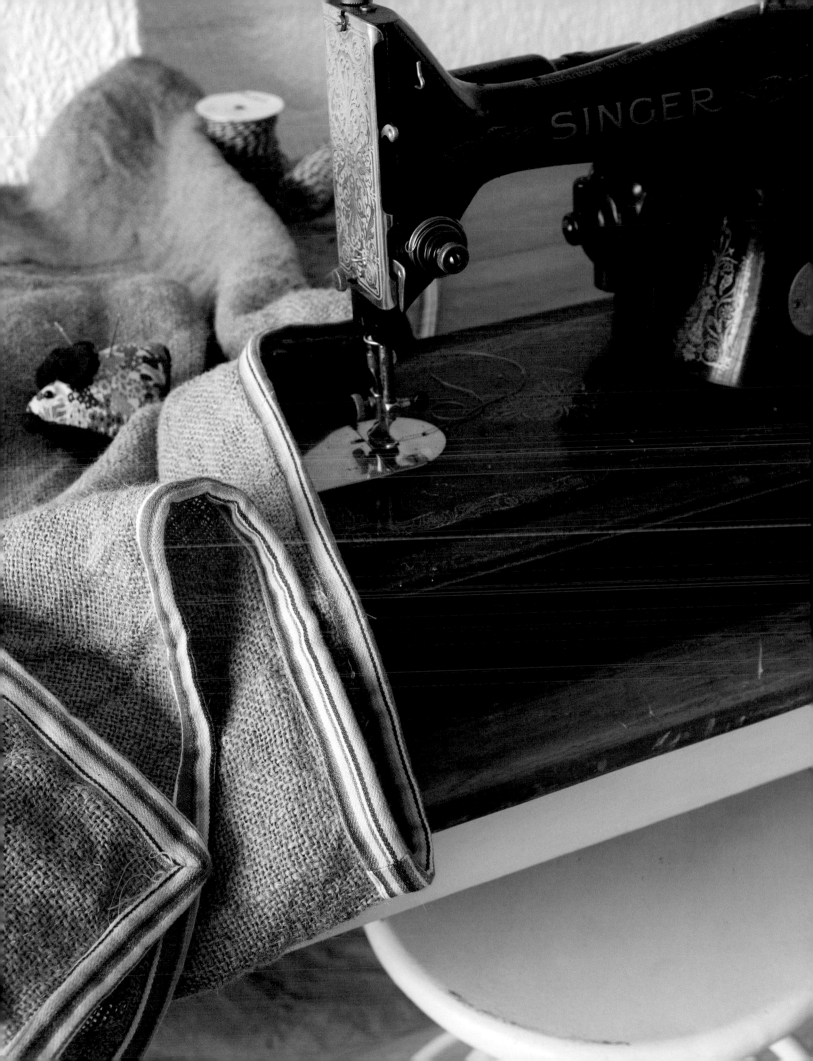

Vintage Lace Curtain

When op shopping, I always pick up any sweet little hankies and embroidered linen I might find. I love to use them to wrap small presents, or once I've collected enough of them, they can always be pieced together to make a tablecloth or curtain.

For this little sheer curtain, I also added in some designer cuttings from Schumacher to prevent the overall design from becoming too 'granny chic'.

1. Simply arrange the pieces to a size that will fit the area to be curtained, pin and sew.
2. Add a few little lace ribbons to the top of the curtain to enable it to be tied to a rod or wire.

Retro Sheet Curtain

If you're lucky enough to find a vintage sheet or tablecloth the same size as your window, it's extremely easy to convert it into a curtain as the edges have already been hemmed for you.

Simply turn the top over once, then pin and sew along one straight line, to create a rod pocket for a curtain rod to slide through.

Note: though these '70s sheets were found still in their retro pack, don't be opposed to using second-hand sheets, after all we use them every time we stay in a hotel. Just, make sure they're stain-free and wash thoroughly in very hot water (drying in the hot sun or in a hot dryer will also banish any germs).

How to hang

Regular rods are probably the easiest to use. Purchase an inexpensive rod set (that includes the brackets and screws) and install. As a general guide, mount the rod about 10 cm/4 in (or a hand's width) above and to the sides of the architrave (window frame). You'll need a power drill for some substrates but plasterboard walls can be drilled into by hand (ask your local hardware store if you're unsure).

Painting Tips

Chalk paints:

Chalk paints make painting furniture a breeze, as they require very little preparation and have a super quick drying time. This means you can literally transform a piece in one afternoon. They leave a lovely chalky finish (hence the name), which is highly suited to relaxed beach, shabby and vintage interiors.

The downside is the finish is matt, so will mark easily if you don't seal it.

Acrylic paints:

You'll need to spend more time preparing pieces before you paint, if you choose to use an acrylic paint, and the drying time is longer but the end result will be hardier and you won't need to seal it (choose between a low-sheen, satin or gloss finish—the higher the sheen, the hardier it'll be).

Use acrylic paint for pieces that will receive a fair amount of wear and tear.

Chalkboard paints:

Not to be confused with chalk paints, chalkboard paints are paints that you literally make chalkboards with. Excellent as a feature wall paint in a kitchen as you can quickly scribble a shopping list on it or see our project on how to create a vintage framed chalkboard for an office or child's room (see opposite).

Chalk Paint Vintage Frame

Since chalk paints require very little preparation, this frame was given a quick clean (with an old toothbrush to help get into all the ornate crevices) and then, once dry, given three coats of paint (often two coats would be enough, but I was going from dark to white, so needed three).

1. To create a memo board as we did in the picture, simply add strips of elastic to the back of your frame.

Vintage Frame Chalkboard

You'll often find paintings you don't love in beautiful old frames. A really simple way to update these, without having to pull them apart, is to simply turn them into pretty chalkboards. Just ensure the existing art is unwanted and/or not valuable!

1. Protect the frame by covering it in masking tape.
2. Apply a good quality primer to the picture and leave to dry.
3. Follow with two coats of specialty chalkboard paint.

Note: chalkboard paint doesn't necessarily need to be black or classroom green; it now comes in a whole range of colours, including hot pink and orange!

il gelato al cioccolato é buonissimo

Child's Stool, Dipped and Decaled

Acrylic paint is a little hardier than (unsealed) chalk-finish paint, therefore ideal to use on children's furniture.

Dipped

To create little 'dipped' legs on tables, stools or chairs, sand and paint the piece in your chosen main colour.

1. Carefully apply masking tape, wrapping it firmly around each leg at the point where you want the legs to be 'dipped' to.
2. Apply two to three coats of paint (allowing the paint to dry between coats).
3. Remove the masking tape.

Decaled

To add a little vintage picture to a piece of furniture, source an image by hunting through old children's book at your local charity store.

1. Cut out the picture and use craft glue to attach it to the piece of furniture.
2. Seal with a clear sealer.

'Vintage' Bedside

Chalk paint, with its soft, 'chalky' finish, is ideal for creating a worn vintage appearance. For this project you need to apply two different coloured coats of paint, and so the fast drying time associated with this paint also helps.

The main colour will be the top coat, which will be sanded back just a little to expose a layer of base coat. In this instance, I've used a pretty pale blue over white.

1. Thoroughly clean the piece.
2. Paint it with your chosen base coat. Leave to dry.
3. Apply one or two coats of your chosen main colour. Leave to dry.
4. Lightly sand the surface to reveal some of the base coat.
5. Seal with beeswax (for a soft, tactile finish) or in a clear acrylic (for a hardier finish).

Note: for a more authentic looking finish, only sand back where a piece might naturally receive wear and tear, which is generally around the edges.

Outdoor Cane Sofa

Woven cane sofas and chairs can be purchased inexpensively secondhand and can be given a new lease of life with a coat of white paint and some fresh cushions. As cane is a natural material, it'll need to be sealed if it's to be used outside (use acrylic paint for this), and will need to be kept in a semi-protected spot.

1. Thoroughly clean the frame; using a toothbrush to get rinto the crevices.
2. Apply a quality primer.
3. Once dry, apply two or three coats of acrylic paint.
4. Meanwhile, if new cushion inserts are needed, use pieces of large paper to make up templates of the old cushions, and take to your local foam supplier to have a piece cut to size (ask for outdoor foam).
5. Choose an outdoor fabric and sew or order new covers. We used 'Swaying Palms' by Tommy Bahama.

Ribbon Lampshade

If re-covering a lampshade in the traditional fashion seems a little tricky, this little ribbon shade is much easier to do. All you need is a new or salvaged drum or empire-style shade and enough ribbon to cover it.

1. Cut lengths of contrasting ribbon just longer than the height of the shade.
2. Using fabric glue, attach the end of the first ribbon to the inside top of the shade, stretch it firmly down the side of the shade and then glue to the inside base of the shade.
3. Keep attaching the ribbons one by one, always alternating the colours and overlapping them slightly until you have covered your whole shade.

Note: to avoid glare, always cover your shade well. Resist the temptation of an industrial style naked frame (unless it's for decoration only). The light emitted from a well-shaded lamp is more flattering and easier on your eyes.

Crystal Decanter Pendant

Beautiful old crystal and glass decanters can be affordably sourced from charity shops and converted into pendant fittings with just a little help.

1. Take the decanter to a local glazier and ask for them to carefully cut the base out of the decanter.
2. Ask an electrician to supply a cord set and install.

Note: You can convert all sorts of vessels into pendants including hand-turned timber bowls, ceramic pots, retro tins, to name a few

Painted Woven Pendant

Update inexpensive natural woven pendants by painting (or even staining) them in a colour of your choice. This tends to make them look more expensive, or at the very least more unique.

1. Apply masking tape to the inner lighting components and cord to protect them.
2. Suspend your pendant from a tree or clothesline to make painting easier.
3. Apply two coats of paint.

Note: Pendants can be spray-painted or alternatively, use a little paintbrush to 'cut into' crevices.

China and Crystal Cake Stand

A decadent afternoon tea is one of life's sweetest and most affordable little pleasures. Dress your table with fine bone china teapots and cups, vintage silverware and a lovely old embroidered tablecloth—all of which can be found for a song at a local charity store.

An old tiered cake stand is a little harder to find, but you can make your own in minutes. Simply collect a couple of crystal glasses and a few china plates and saucers – and secure together with non-toxic craft glue.

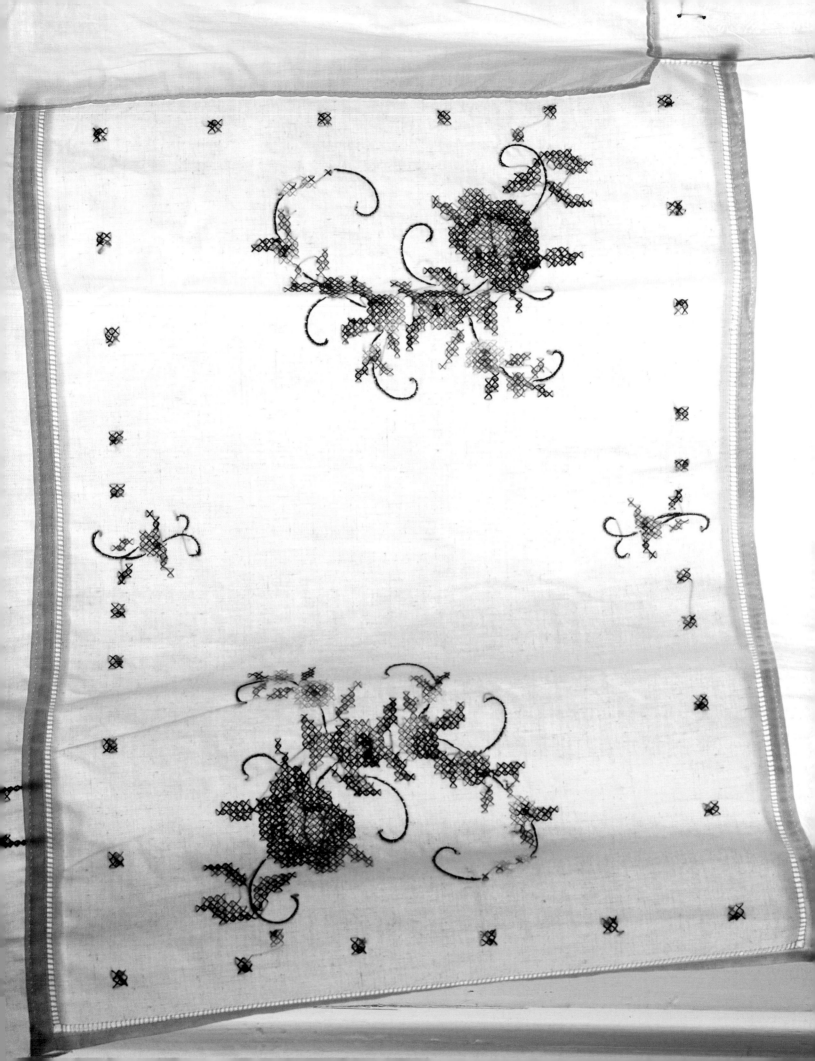

Tea Canister Herb Plant

Almost any container can be turned into a pot plant holder – you just need to punch a couple of drainage holes into the base.

A cute idea for tea drinkers is to plant your favourite herbal tea plant into an old tea canister. To create the drainage holes, turn the can upside down and use a hammer and nail (or a bradawl, which is a special pointed tool used for punching small holes) to tap holes into the base of the can. Fill with potting mix and the herbal plant of your choice. Place the lid under the can to act as a drainage tray.

Note: To make fresh herbal tea, simply pluck a few leaves and steep in boiling water for 10–15 minutes.

Christmas Decorating Ideas

For a more thoughtful, heartfelt Christmas, consider making decorations from vintage pieces or everyday items you might have lying around the home. Here a just a few ideas:

Jam jar candleholders

Old glass jars make super sweet, simple and safe candleholders. Simply fill the jars with water, add a few sprigs of rosemary and float tea lights on top.

Gingerbread Christmas Tree

Spicy gingerbread cookies are so deliciously Christmassy. To create a tree-shaped centrepiece all you need is a good gingerbread recipe and a set of 5 or 6 star-shaped cookie cutters in a range of sizes. Cut out and bake two cookies in each size. Once cool, carefully stack together, using a dab of icing to secure. Sprinkle liberally with icing (confectioners') sugar.

Gingerbread Cookies

I love this gingerbread recipe; it's originally from my favourite little cookbook, *The Perfect Cookbook* by David Herbert, though I've played with it over the years and it's changed a little. I prefer honey over golden syrup and use nutmeg and cinnamon rather than mixed spice – but it's beautiful whichever way you do it, so just use whatever ingredients you have at hand.

125 g (4 ½ oz) butter
60 ml/2 fl oz/¼ cup honey
75 g/2 ½ oz/⅓ cup of raw or coconut sugar
225 g8 oz/2 cups of plain (all-purpose) wholemeal (whole wheat) flour
30 g/1 oz/¼ cup of self-raising (self-rising) flour
1 teaspoon bicarbonate of soda
1 tablespoon ground ginger
1 teaspoon cinnamon
1 teaspoon nutmeg
Pinch of sea salt
1 egg, lightly beaten

1. Melt the butter, honey and sugar in a small pan over a low heat. Remove from the heat and leave to cool.
2. Sift the flours, bicarbonate of soda, spices and salt into a large bowl. Add the melted butter mixture and the beaten egg and mix well.
3. Tip out onto a lightly floured surface and knead until smooth. Pop into a plastic container and refrigerate for 30 minutes.
4. Place between two sheets of baking paper and roll out with a rolling pin to a thickness of 5 mm. Cut out shapes with cookie cutters and bake at 160°C/325°F/Gas mark 3 for 8–10 minutes, or until firm. Allow to cool on a wire rack.

Scrap Fabric Wreath

To make a simple, pretty wreath in the colour palette of your choice, all you need is a rattan or wire ring (available from craft stores, or you can make your own from jewellery/garden wire) and scraps of vintage or remnant fabric. We used Liberty 'Lodden' for our main fabric. Cut your fabric into small strips, approximately 2 x 14 cm/¾–6½ in each, and tie firmly onto your hoop until the entire hoop is covered. Attach a ribbon and hang.

Christmas table tip: Buy vintage, you'll get more decadence for your dollar. Bone china, crystal and real silver can all be picked up for a song at a local charity store.

Flower School

As a stylist I often work with flowers, but was originally lacking in any formal training so asked my friend, florist Christine Campbell (from Wild at Heart Flowers) for the following tips. They're extremely simple but helped me enormously, so I hope they help you too.

Basic Arrangement

This is a very simple but effective three-step method to create an arrangement. Firstly, gather your flowers. You'll need foliage (greenery), a feature flower and some fillers (something sweet and light to fill in the gaps).

Start with your foliage. This forms the shape of your arrangement and gives the other flowers something to rest against. Place in your vase in a criss-cross formation.

Add your feature flower, this is your most beautiful flower, something with a lush head works well (here I've used roses). Add blooms in threes, so you'll need 3, 6 or 9 blooms depending on the size of your arrangement.

Lastly, fill any gaps by gently slipping in your filler, usually something with much smaller flowerheads than your feature (think baby's breath and Queen Anne's lace but try something less traditional).

We used:
Foliage: Eriostemon (a flowering foliage).
Feature: Rose (a classic feature).
Filler: Jonquil (light and pretty).

Notes: Always use a clean, bacteria-free vase. Florists tend to clean vases out with bleach, but use hot, soapy water followed by a white vinegar rinse if you'd prefer not to use chemicals.

Trim all leaves and shoots away from stems, so that only the naked stems are emerged in the water. This will help to keep the water clean.

Refresh with fresh water every few days.

One Bloom, Four Ways

To show you just how versatile a flower can be, I've bought a pretty selection of stocks and displayed them in four different ways:

In tall vases: Trim stems so the heads of the flowers just reach over the top of the vase. Use a vase that splays out at the top, as it shows off the flowers better (and allows you to fit more in).

In shorter vessels: Clip stems down to size, again so the heads only just pop over the top of the vase, but this time, also snip off the pointy tops of the heads to form lovely rounded blooms that better suit a shorter vase (and mimic hydrangeas).

In bud vases: Gather a collection of sweet little vessels and pop a single bloom in each.

As a garland: Simply string together any leftover blooms using a regular needle and strong thread. Thread through the base of the bud. Tie a knot after each bud to keep them separated.

Foliage in a Basket

This is a lovely way to display flowering foliage and the really great thing about it is you can usually forage for foliage for free in your own back yard, or perhaps in a kind neighbour's garden.

All you need to do is clip off a branch or two and place in a water-filled yogurt pot. Place the pot into your basket. If it needs a little more support, wrap an old hand towel snugly around the base of the pot.

We used:
Camelias, which are extremely fresh and pretty, and last for weeks.

Architectural Branches

The benefit of using foliage over cut flowers is their longevity. Keep the water clean and the stems will last for weeks. Buying beautiful flowering foliage, such as the cherry blossom we used here, can be expensive, but, at the right time of year, you may be able to clip something judiciously straight off a tree.

Display a couple of branches in vessels of differing heights to obtain a sleek architectural look. At night you might like to (safely) place tea lights at the base to create beautiful sculptural shadows.

Note: Check the neck of your vases. Narrow vase necks will make flowers point straight up and are best suited to more architectural-style arrangements, they're not so great for lovely 'floppy' arrangements. Medium vase necks are perfect for most arrangements. Wide vase necks need a lot of flowers, so are best for big arrangements.

Say No to Chemicals

We introduce so many unnecessary chemicals into our homes with the cleaning products that we use. Yet almost everything in our homes can be cleaned with a combination of white vinegar, baking soda (bicarbonate of soda) and hot, soapy water. Add some essential oils to your shopping list, including tea tree, lavender, clove and eucalyptus and you'll be able to deal with dirt, grease, unwanted bacteria and even insects with ease.

Cleaning tips

- Fill a couple of spray bottles with white vinegar, a little water and a dozen drops of eucalyptus oil. Keep one in the bathroom and one in the kitchen to clean toilets, benches, basins, mirrors and other surfaces.
- Clean floors with hot water, white vinegar and a few drops of tea tree oil.
- Clean windows with soapy hot water and rinse with water and white vinegar.
- Sprinkle baking soda (bicarbonate of soda) and a couple of drops of water into teacups and rub to instantly remove tea and coffee stains. This also works well for cleaning sinks and stove tops.
- Use a mixture of clove oil and water in place of bleach to deal with mould.
- Once or twice a year steam clean you rugs, carpets, mattresses and upholstery.

Acknowledgements

With heartfelt thanks to…

John Downs, Anastasia Kariofyllidis and Elouise van Riet-Gray for their truly beautiful photography.

To all the friends and clients who kindly allowed us to photograph their homes; Natalie Holt, Sonya Horsburgh, Niccy Mockbridge, Tess Wells, Ellie Ramsay, Sandy Palmer, Erica Davis, Carla Burns, Briony McNeil, Susan Gallagher, Sue Corley, Sarah Dunlop, Sam Emanuel, Simone Georgette, Jody Marsden, Prue Daly, Rachael Turner and Vanessa Scoon (and their partners and families).

A very big thank you to Lazybones for their divine bed linen and locations (locations shots include pages 19, 46 and opposite) and Paint Me White (11, 70).

And also to Absolutely Fabrics, Blake & Taylor, Sachs and Cornish, Found. home & vintage, My Beautiful Things, Lily's Secret, Vanilla Pod, Grass Tree Kitchen, Front Porch Properties, Bisque Interiors, Woolloongabba Antique Centre, Fabric Traders and Taylor-King Gallery for props and/or location assistance.

Thank you to Heidi Wibaux (Found. home & vintage) and Tanya Voll (Clove Lane) for their painting help; decorator Tess Wells (Absolutely Fabrics), Wendy Bryett and my mum, Beth Wilcox for their sewing skills; Briony and Andrew for their woven pendant project; and Chris Campbell (Wild at Heart Flowers) for sharing her floral arranging skills.

To the lovely Diane Ward and the team at New Holland; and Queensland Homes, Choices Flooring and Australian Country who kindly gave me permission to republish some of my work.
And lastly a big thank you to my little models Scarlett, Lily, Lottie and Imogen.

Photography credits:
John Downs; Pages 6/7, 11, 17, 19, 25, 26, 27/28, 34, 37, 45, 46, 48, 52, 53, 56, 58, 59 (top left, bottom right), 64, 70, 75 (bottom right), 78, 79, 80/81, 90, 93, 103, 111, 112, 115, 117/118, 121, 122, 123, 125, 126.
Anastasia Kariofyllidis; Pages 8, 12, 20, 22, 33, 35, 38, 39, 40, 41, 49, 54, 55, 59 (top right, bottom left), 62, 69, 73, 74, 75 (bottom left), 76/77, 89, 99, 100, 108, 128/129.
Elouise van Riet-Gray; Pages 1, 15, 30, 42, 51, 61, 63, 82, 85, 86, 94, 97, 104, 107, 116, 131, 132, 134, 135, 137, 138, 141, 143 and author image.
All photos styled by Tahn Scoon.

Art credit:
'The Ballet' by Lisa Taylor-King, Page 43

First published in 2015 by New Holland Publishers Pty Ltd
London • Sydney • Auckland

The Chandlery Unit 009 50 Westminster Bridge Road London SE1 7QY United Kingdom
1/66 Gibbes Street Chatswood NSW 2067 Australia
5/39 Woodside Ave Northcote, Auckland 0627 New Zealand

www.newhollandpublishers.com

A record of this book is held at the British Library and the National Library of Australia.

ISBN 9781742576343

Managing Director: Fiona Schultz
Production Director: Olga Dementiev
Publisher: Diane Ward
Designer: Lorena Susak
Editor: Simona Hill
Printer: Toppan Leefung Printing Ltd

10 9 8 7 6 5 4 3 2 1

Keep up with New Holland Publishers on Facebook
www.facebook.com/NewHollandPublishers